Montessori and Your Child

Montessori and Your Child

A Primer for Parents

Terry Malloy

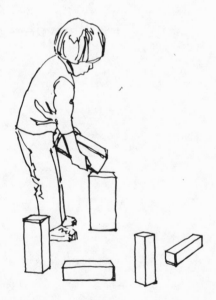

SCHOCKEN BOOKS • NEW YORK

Drawings by Paul Berkow

This is dedicated
to the one I love.

(M. S. A.)

Contents

This handbook is written for
parents of young children,
especially of those between
2½ and 6 years of age.
Its purpose is to help them
understand and assist in
the growth of their child.

In the spirit of respect for
each individual child, "he"
and "she" have been used
on alternate pages.

PART ONE:

WHAT IS YOUR CHILD REALLY LIKE?

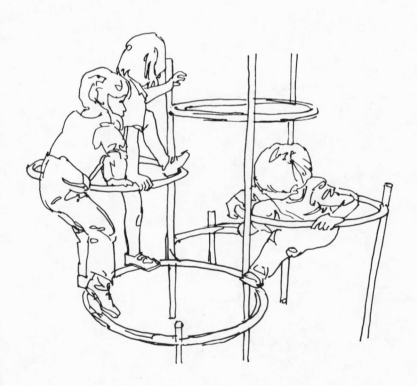

Have you ever been annoyed because someone was rushing you?

Your child's natural rhythm is much slower than yours.

He does not have your adult sense of time. To him, things do not seem so urgent. He cannot plan for the future as you do. Your child's life exists for him in the present moment.

Do you feel resentful when someone
else tells you what to do?

A desire to be independent is
one of the strongest
drives in your child.

While she needs and wants your
help and guidance, a young
child has a very strong urge
to be independent, that is,
to do as much as she can
for herself and by herself.

Have you ever experienced the
difference between reading or
hearing about something and
then actually doing it yourself?

The young child learns through
using his senses.

Your child's senses are very
strong; smells, sounds, textures,
colors and tastes are all new
and exciting to him. He learns
about the world through his
physical contact with the
things in it.

Do you remember how it feels when someone you care for hurts your feelings?

A young child is very sensitive.

Your child has not yet learned to control her feelings as an adult can. She feels everything very directly and strongly. Nor has she learned to express her feelings as adults do. Her hurt feelings may remain buried inside her or may express themselves in disruptive, angry behavior.

Do you think you could learn to play tennis by reading a book, by watching others, or by having someone tell you about the game?

Young children learn by doing.

While adults can learn some things by reading, watching or hearing information, your child learns almost completely by doing things himself. He is still largely developing his body and his mind and he does this by using them.

Do you feel good when your surroundings are neat and well-organized?

Your child has a very strong sense of order.

She needs to live in an environment where things have their proper places. She wants some regular routines in her life to give order to her day.

A young child can be deeply disturbed by disorder; she may even cry when something is out of place, although she does not know the cause of her distress.

Have you ever been hurt when a friend, perhaps unknowingly, insulted you?

Your child has a strong sense of personal dignity.

He does not yet have your adult sense of perspective. He cannot brush off a personal hurt or analyze or explain it to himself. To your child, any attack on his personal dignity is a rejection of him as a person; it is someone saying he is, in some way, worthless or a failure.

Was there ever a person you
admired and tried to
be like?

Your child learns mainly through
imitating the adults in
her life who are closest
to her.

A young child's parents are the
models whom she imitates in
learning about life. Her
attitude is much like one
who worships an idol. She
copies many adult actions
and attitudes and also stores
much of what she sees for
later use as she matures.

Have you ever felt really
good about something new
that you learned?

A natural urge to grow, to
expand and to develop is
the basic drive in the
young child.

All living things must grow in
some way if they are to
stay alive. To your child,
the world is totally new and
must be explored. Each new
thing that he discovers and
learns about helps him in
his growth toward adulthood.

Can you remember the pleasure
of learning something new
and doing it over and
over again?

Repetition is an important way
through which your child learns.

Quite naturally, she often repeats
some activity many times. In
this way, she can master it.
She also repeats things because
they are so new and interesting
to her. She is fascinated by
the fact that she can do it,
that she is making something
happen, that she can control
the world around her.

Did you ever wake up with aching muscles after having tried a new physical activity?

The muscles of the young child are largely undeveloped.

Your child needs many years of growth and of using his muscles in order for them to develop. This occurs in different stages as your child's body grows and changes. There are certain things a young child simply <u>cannot</u> do because his body is not developed enough.

Have you ever noticed That when
you really concentrate you
learn better and faster
and even enjoy it more?

Your child has a very strong
natural ability to concentrate
on one particular thing at
a time.

A child's intense ability to
concentrate allows her to
involve herself entirely in
learning something. If she
is not interrupted, her
concentration can last for
long periods of time.

Have you ever felt really
satisfied because you did
a job well?

The young child actually prefers
work over play.

Given a choice, your child will
prefer to do "real" work such
as cleaning, cooking or gardening
rather than "play". Children
have a deep love for work and
they long to share in the adult
world of doing meaningful, necessary
tasks. They want to participate
in family life and help to care
for themselves and their environment.

Did you ever feel that no one really understands you the way you understand yourself?

Your child is "self-centered"; that is, she is mainly aware of her own feelings and desires and has not yet developed a true sense of feeling for other people.

A true sense of understanding and being considerate of others is an adult quality that takes many years to develop. The newborn baby knows only herself. Gradually, naturally, a child develops an awareness of others through her many years of social contacts.

Did you ever feel a little sorry when you finished making something because doing it was so much fun?

Your child is mainly interested in the process of doing things; he is not very concerned with the end result.

Although the finished product may please a child and give him a sense of success and accomplishment, his real pleasure is in the activity of work itself. The adult concern with a future goal does not preoccupy the young child; he is totally involved in the present moment of what he is doing.

Have you ever felt you were "too old" to learn something new?

The young child has certain "sensitive periods" when it is easiest for her to learn some particular thing.

Sensitive periods come at slightly different times in a child's life, but all children have them. It is important for adults to recognize these times and provide the child with proper assistance so she can learn each skill or concept at the time that is best for her.

(See table of sensitive periods in Appendix)

PART TWO:

WHAT DOES YOUR
CHILD NEED?

Your child needs love, warmth and security.

The young child is dependent on adults for many things, but the most important is a sense of being cared for.

Moments of physical closeness, a smile, a kiss and a hug to express the love you feel for your child are vital for his development. Such signs of affection should always be natural and never be forced upon a child.

Your child needs to be
treated with respect.

A young child, with her strong
sense of personal dignity and
her deep sensitivity, needs to
be treated with respect.

Your child needs to be listened
to by the adults in her world.
She needs to see that her
own feelings and ideas are
important and worthy of
consideration. She needs to feel
that she is included as a
respected member of her family.

This does not mean that she
needs to "get her way";
your child does not really
want to rule, only to
share.

Your child needs understanding.

Although you may not always agree with him, your young child needs to feel that you understand him.

Taking time to listen, to consider and perhaps to change in response to his feelings and ideas helps your child build feelings of self-respect and increases his love and respect for you.

Your child needs freedom to explore her world.

Your child needs open space, both indoors and outdoors, in which she can move about freely.

Your child needs freedom to learn by himself.

He needs objects in his environment that he can freely handle and manipulate without adult interference.

Your child needs sensible rules and limits in her life that are enforced fairly and consistently.

Your child is relatively inexperienced and needs the benefit of your knowledge. She also needs to learn how to live happily with other people.

Sensible, flexible rules and limits that she can accept and follow easily are important. They should be agreed upon by both parents, presented to the child and enforced firmly and cheerfully. They give your child a sense of security in her environment and in her relationships with others.

Your child needs much time to explore his world and to do things for himself.

Since a young child's sense of time differs from that of an adult, he should not be rushed.

By being allowed to explore his world slowly, your child can learn things at his own natural pace. In the same way, he requires sufficient time to allow him to do things for himself in his own way without adult interference.

Your child needs an orderly
environment and regular
routines in her life.

To the very young child, the
world is a confusing mass of
unknown things. As she grows,
she explores her world and
learns many things about it.

In order to make sense of it
all, your child needs an orderly
environment and atmosphere
in which to live and grow.
Parents who provide such order
for their child help her to
develop in a natural, healthy
way so that she can
understand and learn to
deal with life.

Your child needs to have many opportunities for success in his life.

Whenever your young child succeeds at something, he has a sense of personal worth; he has also furthered the development of his mind and body.

Adults can provide guidance that will allow a child to experience as many successes as possible and, in contrast, as few failures as possible.

(See suggestions for parents in Appendix)

Your child needs frequent praise and encouragement.

Honest praise and encouragement from adults help your child to feel good about herself. She feels a sense of personal worth and is motivated to continue her efforts to learn.

A child does not require a great deal of praise or false enthusiasm—these can actually harm her.

But a few, genuine, warm words or gestures of appreciation for her efforts and her personal qualities are very important for your child.

Your child needs to find out
"who he is" and how he
is unique.

Each of us is different in
some ways from everyone else.
A sense of how he is unique
is important to the growth
of your child.

He needs to feel special in
some way and to have
this quality recognized by
others, especially his parents.

Your child needs human companionship.

The young child needs more than just the presence of other people. She needs to do things with them, to interact with them.

Your child wants you to respect her as an individual and include her in your life. She also needs other adults and children around her. This helps her to learn to deal with and enjoy different kinds of people.

Your child needs a stimulating environment.

The young child shows limitless curiosity. He needs to have a stimulating environment that he can explore freely and learn from.

This environment is created to a large extent by parents. They can provide proper materials in the home and also take their child to interesting places outside the home.

As always, a good balance is important; overstimulation must be avoided. Your child needs time to fully explore something new before he is ready for the next new thing.

Your child needs the right environment to develop her mind and body.

Since your child learns mainly through her senses in growing levels of complexity, she needs an environment that matches her particular needs at any given time.

When you know what materials to provide her with, your child's growth and learning will occur naturally and effortlessly; she will actually teach herself with only a minimum of guidance from the adult world.

PART THREE :

HOW CAN YOU HELP
YOUR CHILD?

Treat your child with respect and consideration.

Listen to your child when he wants to tell you something. Try to bend down or sit so that you are on his level and there is eye contact between you.

Try to understand your child's ideas and feelings and consider them in your family life. Remember that things which seem trivial to you can be very important to your child.

Include your child in family plans and decisions whenever possible. Help him feel that he is an important member of his family.

Be flexible in your relationship
with your child.

Young children grow and change
very rapidly. Your child needs
a flexible relationship with
her parents so that rules and
regulations can be modified
to suit her changing needs.

Decisions to make such
changes should be made by
both parents and should
be discussed with the
child and clearly explained
to her.

Provide your child with definite structures that still leave room for freedom.

Your child needs the security and guidance that firm, sensible rules provide.

He should be informed of all rules and given brief explanations when necessary. If rules are carefully thought out and regularly enforced, your child will usually accept them without difficulty.

If a child is greatly unhappy about a rule, further thought should be given to it and possible changes made if parents see fit. Very often, family discussions including your child are a good way to handle this.

Consider your child's slower sense of time.

When your child is near you, try to keep your movements slow and deliberate. Plan ahead so that you will not have to rush your child - tell her well in advance of an event, such as going shopping, so that she can prepare by herself at her own speed.

Plan to spend some time each day in some activity with your child that will be leisurely and enjoyable for both of you.

Allow time for your child to complete each activity that she begins. If an activity has become extremely complex or tiring, you may assist her in completing it - but never do it for her.

Don't do anything for your child that he can do himself.

Allow and encourage your child to do things that he is ready and able to do.

Teach him to feed himself, dress himself, do simple chores such as dusting, gathering leaves and watering plants. Demonstrate each activity to him in a slow, simple manner with as few words as possible, and let him try himself. Do not correct mistakes; if a child is not ready for some activity, show him again another time.

Give your child time to learn and to practice each activity. Allow him to help at home whenever possible— suggest, do not ever force.

Children enjoy such work and will usually participate cheerfully. Do not redo your child's work in his presence; accept what he is able to do graciously.

Provide your child with freedom to choose whenever possible.

Respect for her individuality and need for freedom are shown by parents who allow their child some genuine choices.

For example, you may ask your child if she wants vanilla or chocolate ice cream; if she wants to play with a friend or go to the park; if she wants to wear her blue dress or her red one; if she wants to put the napkins or the glasses on the table.

Learning to make such choices is an important part of growing up.

Give your child as many opportunities for success as possible.

Because you know your own child, you can usually tell what he can and cannot do. Present him with activities that he will be able to perform without too much difficulty or error. Help him by showing him what to do in a careful, simple, slow way, and then allow him to try for himself.

Praise your child's successes, ignore any failures, and remove any materials that you see are still too difficult for him. You can often be guided by the interest your child shows in something; such real interest is a powerful motivation for learning.

Try to be positive in your
dealings with your child.

Find another way to tell her things
so you can avoid using such words
as "don't", "can't", "must not",
"shouldn't" and "wrong".

If, for example, your child is
pounding her fists on the table,
explain calmly that the table is for
eating and that she can use clay
for pounding - then direct her to
the clay.

If your child has been wiping a
table and has overlooked a spot,
you need only point to it, or
perhaps say "one more spot
and the table will be perfect".

Negative words make your child feel
badly about herself; positive, helpful
reactions help her feel
independent and successful.

Use precise language when speaking to your child.

You can greatly assist your child's ability to express himself clearly by using careful speech around him.

A young child is continually learning new words and expanding his vocabulary and his powers of communication.

Help your child learn the names of the things in his world by using them yourself. Instead of "please give me that thing over there", try to say "please give me the red book on the end table".

Whenever possible, let your child
use real objects.

Toys that look like real objects, but
don't work as they do are
frustrating to the young child and
only serve to confuse and sometimes
anger her. She may feel that she
is not "good" enough to use the
real thing.

Your child prefers to use the
objects she sees adults handling.
A child-sized dust pan and broom,
a small sponge and wash tub,
a little rake and hoe are excellent
learning devices for your child.

She can perform real tasks, help in
family chores and activities, and
have a genuine sense of
accomplishment as she learns
and performs meaningful work.

Think of yourself as a model that your child is going to copy and learn from.

Your young child spends much of his time in your presence. He learns from watching you and imitating you.

If you want your child to be loving, honest, orderly or gentle it is best to be like this yourself.

When a child is continually scolded or spanked, he learns to behave this way toward others.

Parents should be aware of the tremendous power they have in shaping their child's life and personality.

Provide your child with opportunities to be with other children.

Your child needs and enjoys the presence of other children, both her age and of other ages.

Before the age of three, children seldom communicate directly with one another or show awareness of others as separate and different individuals.

However, some exposure to other children, even before three, can help your child learn to get along with others and enjoy their company.

After three or four, such contacts with other children assist her intellectual growth and are essential for her social development.

Provide your child with a stimulating environment suited to his needs.

Parents who know their child's abilities at any given time can provide materials and activities that will greatly assist his growth and development.

Young children can be given a small tub of water and some plastic bottles, sponges and strainers to work with; also useful are a sandbox, pail, shovel and watering can; shells and pebbles for sorting and counting; playdough and cookie cutters, rolling pin and buttons- these are a few suggestions.

Provide your child with his own work area or table; give him a few, sturdy objects that are his to work with. Introduce new objects slowly and give him time to become completely familiar with them before you give him something else.

Books, magazines and teachers can help you choose appropriate materials for your child.

If possible, find a good pre-primary school for your child.

The importance of the years from birth to six in the formation of the adult is now agreed upon by most experts. While it is also agreed that parents and home life are the most vital influences in a young child's life, a good pre-primary school can play an important part in your child's growth.

Trained professionals can often provide specific kinds of help not available in the home; they can give a child long-range attention that parents do not always have time for.

Ideally, parents and schools should work together for the benefit of the child. Things learned at school can be reinforced at home; consistency between school and home help your child feel secure and able to understand and deal with her world.

PART FOUR:

WHAT IS THE
MONTESSORI WAY?

The Montessori method can help your child to grow in many ways.

Many of the characteristics of your young child, as mentioned in Part One, were observed by Maria Montessori. Dr. Montessori devised a system of early childhood education that was specifically designed to meet the basic needs of the child, discussed in Part Two. Her methods and exercises are in accord with the suggestions in Part Three.

The Montessori method itself has many aspects and a well-trained Montessori directress has studied and worked a great deal. But the basic ideas and concepts of the system are easily understood by all.

Maria Montessori had a unique understanding of young children.

Born in Italy in 1870, Maria Montessori became the first woman doctor in her country's history. Her early work was with retarded and very poor children; by close observation and experimentation, Dr. Montessori devised a system of education that helped handicapped and deprived children learn as well as normal and average children.

Her methods became world-known and many countries adopted them. Today there is a renewed interest in her system in the United States. Her insights into children and her ideas for helping them grow into healthy, well-rounded adults seem fresh and meaningful today.

The failures of traditional methods of education are becoming more and more obvious. The Montessori way offers a sensible, structured system that allows a child to develop at her own pace, using her own abilities, with the guidance of a trained Montessori directress and the use of specially designed Montessori materials.

The Montessori system has three main parts: the child, the environment and the directress.

At the heart of any system of early childhood education should be the child. Maria Montessori based her entire method on her observations and understanding of the child as he is, not as adults imagine he might or should be.

Dr. Montessori then devised a total environment to help the child develop himself as a total human being.

She saw the role of the teacher as one of directing activity rather than actually teaching, so she preferred to use the name "directress" instead of "teacher".

Montessori sees your child as she really is.

The Montessori method allows your child to learn the way she learns best and easiest: by doing things herself. Basically, she teaches herself.

Within certain limits, your child can choose work that appeals to her own inner interests. She can exercise her sense of freedom and spontaneity; she feels joy and enthusiasm in learning because she is doing what she wants to do instead of what someone else tells her she must do.

Gradually, the child builds a strong sense of independence and self-confidence as her skills increase. The Montessori method is built on your child's natural love of learning and instills a life-long motivation for continuous learning. It helps your child remain in touch with her natural growth and development and avoids forcing her to do anything she is not truly ready for.

The Montessori environment is your child's "teacher."

In a Montessori school, your child teaches himself through his use of the specially designed Montessori materials. These are attractive, generally simple, child-sized materials that are self-correcting; that is, if a child makes an error, he can see it by looking at the material itself. In this way, no adult is needed to point out his mistake and perhaps injure his self-esteem.

Your child learns to work alone and with others in a Montessori school-he can usually make this choice himself. He learns to follow the class "ground rules" and may often remind other children to follow them as well.

Because he can choose his own work and do it at his own pace, your child has many opportunities for success; the Montessori classroom is noncompetitive. He will also have access to plants and animals and will help care for them. The Montessori classroom is an attractive place in which your child can be free from adult domination and can discover his world and build his mind and body.

63

The Montessori classroom covers a number of different areas.

The "Practical Life" area is especially for the very young child (2½-3½) and teaches her how to care for herself and her environment. Here, your child will learn to dress herself by using the dressing frames (buttons, snaps, zipper, buckles, pins, laces, bows, and hooks and eyes), to pour (rice and water), to wash a table, to polish silver and to properly wash her hands, among other things.

The "Sensorial" area allows her to use her senses to learn about the world. Here, your child will learn to judge different heights, lengths, weights, colors, sounds, smells, shapes, and textures.

The language, math, geography and science areas provide your child with aids for her intellectual development. Exercises in body movement assist her physical development and her awareness of her body and what it can do.

Many Montessori schools add such areas as music, art, dancing, sewing, woodworking and foreign languages to further enrich your child's total development.

The Montessori directress has many jobs to do.

Unlike the teacher in a traditional school, the Montessori directress is not the center of the classroom. Instead, she is very often hardly noticeable in the room as the children are working. She has no desk and spends her time working with children at child-sized tables or on the rug.

The directress must be a keen observer of children and needs to have a clear idea of each child's individual level of development. She then determines what materials are best for each child to work with. She guides each individual child in this way and helps him learn the proper use of each material; she then leaves him with it and returns to observing.

The directress interferes only when necessary. She must be flexible and willing to try new ideas to help each child. Your child will come to see the directress as a friendly helper and guide, someone who is there when needed, but mainly someone who helps him to do things for himself.

The Montessori classroom includes children of different ages.

By placing your child in a classroom with children of varying ages (usually between 2½ and 6 years), you are exposing her to a wide range of learning possibilities.

When she first begins school, she will have the benefit of learning from older, more experienced children. Later on, she will be able to help others with learning skills that she has already mastered.

Your child will also learn how to get along socially with a variety of other people.

Each Montessori classroom is different.

Although the Montessori method has very definite structures, it is also flexible and open to individual interpretations.

Because no two people are exactly alike, each Montessori classroom, being largely dependent on the interpretation and abilities of the directress, will be unique.

It is wise for parents to meet with the directress and, if possible, also observe her class in action in order to discover her particular style of Montessori.

The Montessori method is different from all others.

The Montessori method is unique. It is based on a sensible balance between freedom and structure specifically designed for the young child. It provides a pleasant environment with carefully devised materials that meet the child's natural needs. It provides the overall guidance of a thoroughly trained directress.

Montessori gives your child a strong basis, in his most formative years, for developing into a well-rounded, responsible, happy and fulfilled adult.

APPENDIX

Practical Life

Dressing Frames- each frame teaches one particular skill needed in dressing oneself; there are frames with buttons, snaps, zipper, buckles, laces, hooks and eyes, pins and bows.

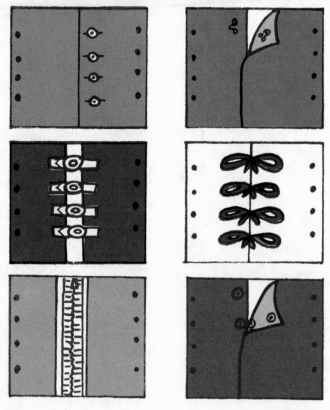

Pouring - pouring exercises help improve coordination and concentration; they include pouring rice and pouring water from one container to another.

Food preparation - exercises include preparing carrots, bananas and apples; they help the child become independent and orderly.

Cleaning exercises - these include shining shoes, polishing silver, sweeping, mopping, washing clothes and washing one's hands; they help the child learn to care for himself and his environment.

Sensorial

The Brown Stair - introduces size differences in two dimensions and teaches concepts of thin, thinner, thinnest and thick, thicker, thickest.

The Pink Tower introduces size differences in three dimensions and helps the child differentiate among big, bigger, biggest and small, smaller, smallest.

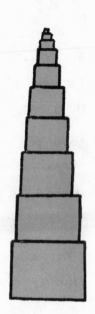

The Red Rods= introduces size difference in one dimension, length; teaches concepts of short, shorter, shortest and long, longer, longest.

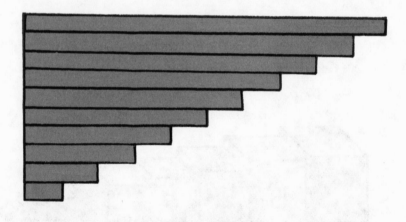

The Color Tablets - in
three sets, the first of
which contains three sets
of primary colors to be
matched (see illustration);
the second set contains
eleven colors for matching
and the third set contains
eight shades of eight
different colors for grading.

These exercises teach names
of colors, increase
awareness of colors and
sharpen the child's ability
to distinguish different
tones.

The Cylinder Blocks- there are four cylinder blocks with ten cylinders each: one set differs only in height, one only in diameter and the other two in both height and diameter. Matching each cylinder to its proper hole teaches size discrimination and develops hand muscles to be used for writing.

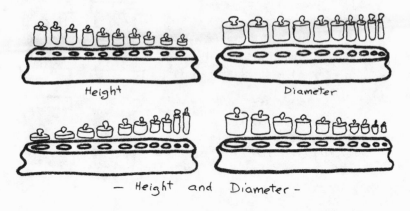

Height

Diameter

— Height and Diameter —

The Knobless Cylinders- each colored set corresponds in size to one cylinder block.

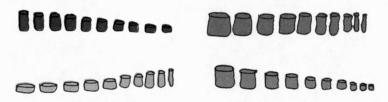

Language

Sandpaper Letters mounted, cut-out sandpaper letters allow the child to learn the shape of each letter through touch and to associate the sound each letter makes with its shape.

Metal Insets there are ten metal insets, each a different geometric shape with a knob for lifting and replacing; tracing the outline of an inset helps prepare the hand and eye for writing.

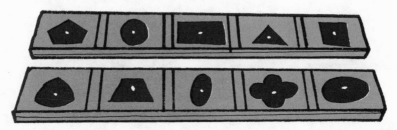

The Sound Boxes- this set consists of two wooden boxes, each containing six cylinders; the sound of each red cylinder matches the sound of one blue cylinder. This exercise sharpens one's ability to distinguish sounds and assists concentration.

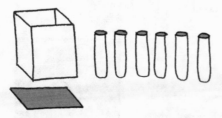

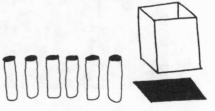

The Geometric Solids- these heavy wooden solids teach shape discrimination as they are seen and handled.

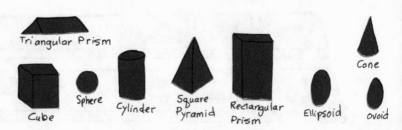

Triangular Prism

Cube   Sphere   Cylinder   Square Pyramid   Rectangular Prism   Ellipsoid   Cone   ovoid

Math

The Red and Blue Rods- this set of ten
rods is the same size as the red
rods, but each rod is divided into
unit sections of red and blue; they
teach the beginning concept of counting
and can also be used for simple adding,
subtracting, multiplying and dividing.

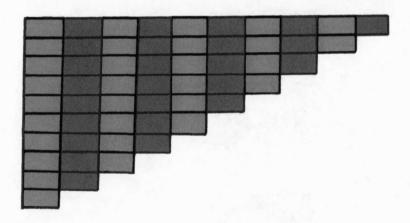

The Spindle Boxes- two boxes divided
into separate compartments and
labelled 0 to 9 are used to teach
counting and the concept of quantity;
the child places the correct number
of rods or wooden sticks in
each compartment.

The Golden Beads - these materials
provide a concrete introduction
to concepts of counting, quantity,
and basic mathematical functions.

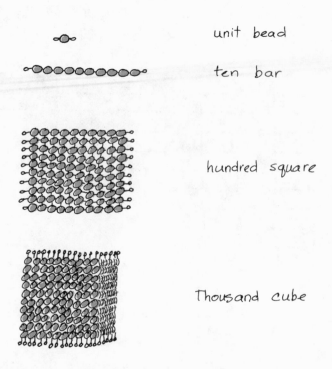

unit bead

ten bar

hundred square

Thousand cube

Other Areas

Puzzle maps- these wooden maps have a small knob on each piece to allow easy manipulation; They are sturdy and attractive and teach names and locations of states, countries and continents as well as basic facts of geography.

Nature cards- different sets of cards teach the parts of a leaf, a flower, and a tree; they build vocabulary and increase awareness of nature.

The bells- These are upright bells that produce different tones when struck with a small mallet; they are used as a sensorial exercise in matching sounds and may also be used to teach the fundamentals of music- scales, composition and playing simple melodies.

The line- most classrooms have a taped circle on the rug or floor that is used for physical exercises that teach balance and coordination.

2. SUGGESTIONS FOR PARENTS

Your Home Environment

1. Buy clothing that your child can put on and take off by himself, such as slacks with elastic waistbands, shirts with large buttons and wide-necked pullovers.

2. Use child-sized furniture in your child's room; give her a low table and mirror, drawers that she can open easily, strong furniture that cannot be easily knocked over, a light chair that she can carry, and low hooks so she can hang up her own clothing.

3. Make your child's room bright, attractive and simple; use easily cleaned surfaces; give him only a few carefully chosen objects in his room at a time.

4. Remove from your child's sight any objects that you value and fear may be damaged.

5. Give your child her own place in other parts of the home for her belongings, such as her towel, toothbrush or coat hanger; you can mark each place with a small piece of colored tape so she can easily recognize it as hers.

6. Give your child his own cleaning materials, such as a small sponge, dust cloth, broom and some polish so he can keep his own room clean.

Activities With Adults

1. Take your child to interesting places such as the library, the post office, local factories, the zoo, museums, children's theatre, the beach, parks, and playgrounds. Discuss what you see there.

2. Let your child share in your chores such as shopping, cooking, cleaning, gardening, woodworking and sewing; give her her own job and the materials she needs to do it well.

3. Share your special interests and hobbies with your child such as knowledge about sports, birds, stamps, plants, animals, knitting, painting, and playing a musical instrument.

4. Give your child magazines for cutting out pictures and discuss the pictures with him; read to your child and tell him stories; show him how to use a tape recorder if you have one.

5. Take your child to visit relatives and friends; keep visits reasonably short and provide something for your child to work with if she becomes restless; encourage grandparents to spend time doing things with your child.

6. Show your child how to care for the plants and animals in your home. Allow him to assume responsibility for their care if this seems appropriate.

Activities For Your Child

1. Give your child a plastic tub of water, some plastic bottles, a funnel, a sponge, a strainer and an apron; allow her to use these things freely and discover what water does; show her how to clean up when she is finished.

2. Provide sand for your child, either in a sandbox or at the beach; give him a watering can to dampen the sand, cookie cutters, a strainer, a funnel, a shovel and a pail; at home, provide a brush and dust pan for him to clean up.

3. Some playdough and cookie cutters, buttons, jar lids and a rolling pin can interest your child for long periods of time; playdough can be easily made at home by mixing

> 1 cup flour
> 1 tablespoon salt
> a few drops of food coloring

and enough water to make a stiff dough; the playdough should be kept in the refrigerator when not in use.

4. Other materials your child will enjoy and learn from include paints, large wooden blocks, books, shells and interesting pebbles and stones. Remember to have a place for each material and to show your child how to use and take care of it herself.

Attitudes and Influences

1. If the father spends his days working away from the home, let your child see him doing some work at home. This is important for your young child who is not able to imagine what his father is doing all day when he is "at work"; he needs to actually <u>see</u> his father doing some kind of work.

2. Prepare your child for new experiences such as getting a haircut, going to the doctor or going to school; explain the visit briefly and calmly and mention it for a few days before you actually go.

3. Answer all your child's questions honestly and simply; never lie to your child.

4. If you are having some difficulty with your child that is disturbing you, ask someone, such as a teacher or a doctor, for help.

3. SENSITIVE PERIODS

The following is a general guide to the times when a young child can best learn specific skills and concepts; they do not always apply to individual children.

Birth- throughout life	-	language
Birth- 3 years	-	sensory experiences
Birth- 1½ years	-	learning through movement
1½ - 3 years	-	development of oral language
1½ - 4 years	-	development of muscular coordination
2 - 4 years	-	concern with order in environment + routines
2 - 6 years	-	music
2½ - 6 years	-	refinement of senses
	-	development of social graces
3 - 6 years	-	sensitivity to adult influences
3½ - 4½ years	-	writing
4 - 4½ years	-	sense of touch
4½ - 5½ years	-	reading

4. THE NORMAL CHILD

The basic goal of the Montessori method is "normalization" of the child so that he becomes well-balanced, spontaneous and able to utilize his capabilities to the fullest. Some of the characteristics of such a child are the following:

1. Ability to concentrate well
2. Sense of personal dignity
3. Independence
4. Self-motivation
5. Love of order
6. Enjoyment of repetition
7. Ability to work alone
8. Self-discipline
9. Desire for freedom of choice
10. Pleasure and fulfillment in work for its own sake; no need for rewards or punishment
11. Obedience
12. Preference for work over play
13. Love of learning

5. OBSERVING A MONTESSORI CLASS

The following questions can help you understand and evaluate what you see in a Montessori classroom.

The Environment

1. Is the room attractive?
2. Are the materials in good condition?
3. Are the materials visible and easily accessible to the children?
4. Does the room seem orderly and well cared for?
5. Do the materials seem to be logically arranged?
6. Is there an outdoor area? a gym?

The Directress

1. Does she seem comfortable and relaxed in the room?
2. Does she speak softly and gently?
3. Does she move slowly and gracefully?
4. Does she seem aware of what is going on in the room?
5. Does she respond to the children appropriately?

6. Does she seem to be in control of the room?
7. Does she treat each child with respect and courtesy?
8. Do the children obey her cheerfully and readily?
9. Does she contribute to keeping order in the room?
10. Does she demonstrate materials clearly and seem aware of the child's response?

The Children

1. Do they seem comfortable in the room?
2. Do they show many periods of involvement with work?
3. Do they follow the ground rules?
4. Do they handle the materials carefully and replace them after use?
5. Do they work well together and alone?
6. Do they ask for help when they need it?
7. Do they follow instructions willingly?
8. Do they seem happy in school?

NOTE

Much of the material in this book has been simplified and shortened.

Those desiring fuller information and more ideas for helping and understanding their child can consult some of the books in the following bibliography.

BIBLIOGRAPHY

I. BOOKS BY MARIA MONTESSORI:

<u>Dr. Montessori's Own Handbook</u>, Schocken Books, New York, 1965.

<u>The Child in the Family</u>, Avon Books, New York, 1970.

<u>The Absorbent Mind</u>, Holt, Rinehart and Winston, 1967; paperback edition Dell, 1967.

<u>The Montessori Method</u>, Schocken Books, New York, 1964.

<u>The Secret of Childhood</u>, Fides Publishers, Inc., Notre Dame, Indiana, 1972.

II. BOOKS BY OTHERS:

<u>Montessori and Music</u>, <u>Rhythmic Activities for Young Children</u>, by Elise Braun Barnett, Schocken Books, Inc., New York, 1972.

<u>Montessori Matters</u>, Sister Mary Matthew Carinato and others, Sisters of Notre Dame de Namur, Ohio Province, 701 E. Columbia Avenue, Cincinnati, Ohio 45215, 1967.

<u>Logical Consequences</u>, by Rudolf Dreikurs and Loren Gray, Meredith Press, New York, 1965.

<u>Ready Your Child For School the Montessori Way</u>, by Lena L. Gitter, St. Meinrad Archabbey, Abbey Press, U.S.A., 1969.

<u>The Montessori Way</u>, by Lena L. Gitter, Special Child Publications, Inc., 4535 Union Bay Place N.E., Seattle, Washington 98105, 1970.

<u>Teaching Montessori in the Home - The Pre-School Years</u>, by Elizabeth G. Hainstock, Random House, N.Y., 1968.

<u>Teaching Montessori in the Home-The School Years</u>, by Elizabeth G. Hainstock, Random House, N.Y., 1971.

Montessori in the Home, Jerome Study Group, 1963. (Available through the American Montessori Society, 175 Fifth Avenue, N.Y., N.Y. 10010.)

Montessori - A Modern Approach, by Paula Lillard, Schocken Books, Inc., 1971; paperback, 1973.

The Hidden Hinge, by Rosa Covington Packard, Fides Publishers, Inc., Notre Dame, Indiana, 1972.

Learning How to Learn, by Nancy Rambusch, Helicon Press, Baltimore, Maryland, 1963.

Maria Montessori - Her Life and Work, by E.M. Standing, New American Library, N.Y., 1962

The Montessori Revolution in Education, by E.M. Standing, Schocken Books Inc., 1966.

<u>Learning With Mother</u>, by Ethel and Harry Wingfield, Wills and Hepworth, Ltd., Loughborough, England, 1970.

III. ARTICLES:

"Lecture on Learning", by Martin Ballard, <u>Teacher Magazine</u>, Feb. 1973, pp. 142-149.

"Do you Know How to Play With Your Child?" by Betty Hoffman, <u>Woman's Day</u>, August 1972, pp. 46, 118, 120.

"Other Side of the Coin", by Ann F. Lucas, <u>NJEA Review</u>, Sept. 1967.

"Questions Parents Ask About Montessori Kindergarten", by Lynn McCormick, Montessori Schools of Omaha Newsletter, April 1971.

"The Montessori Method: Some Recent Research", by Solveiga Miezitis, <u>Interchange</u>, Vol. 2, No. 2, 1971.

"You Can Raise Your Child's I.Q.", by Maya Pines, <u>Reader's Digest</u>, December 1968.

"Montessori on Montessori: A Cautionary Note", by Russell Shaw, <u>The Sign</u>, November 1966.

"A Sober View of Montessori", by Edward Wakin, <u>The Sign</u>, May 1963.

"An Analysis of Excellent Early Educational Practices: Preliminary Report," by Burton L. White, <u>Interchange</u>, Vol. 2, No. 2, 1971.

NOTE: The articles by Miezitis and by White have been reprinted, respectively, in the <u>AMS Bulletin</u> Vol. 10, No. 2 and Vol. 10, No. 3.